MANOEUVRES MADE EASY:
THE McAULAY METHOD
(2004 Edition)

By Gerar

Listen to the advice given by your instructor, or in this book, and you will have every chance of PASSING YOUR DRIVING TEST.

This is also a suitable manual for trainee driving instructors.

Visit us online at www.authorsonline.co.uk

An AuthorsOnLine Book

First Published by Authors OnLine Ltd 2002
This edition update 2004

Copyright © Authors OnLine Ltd

Text Copyright © Gerald McAulay

Graphics and Bookjacket by Rick Jones ©

Editing, Dione M. Coumbe LL.B(Hons.)
Book Publicity Limited, Dover, Kent, England;
www.BookPublicity.co.uk

ISBN 0 7552 0107 8

Authors OnLine Ltd
40 Castle Street
Hertford SG14 1HR
England

This book is also available in e-book format, details of which are available at www.authorsonline.co.uk

To all the people who taught me, from my first driving lesson, instructor training and throughout my driving career.

Gerard McAulay is a Grade 6 Driving Instructor. He decided to write 'Manoeuvres Made Easy' because a large number of his pupils, some from other driving schools, found so much difficulty with them.

The 'McAulay Method' proved how simple these could be.

"I had two pupils, in particular, who just could not deal with roundabouts," Gerard says, "both failed their driving tests twice before coming to me. After showing them my method they had no more problems and both passed their next test."

As a professional driving instructor, coping with nervous and apprehensive pupils, 'McAulay's Method' has been proved practical, being tried and tested successfully on a daily basis. Also included are a wealth of valuable tips for learner and new drivers.

The secret of all manoeuvres is to keep the car SLOW, so that you remain in control of the vehicle.

Index

MANOEUVRES MADE EASY: THE McAULAY METHOD

By Gerard McAulay

Listen to the advice given by your instructor, or in this book, and you will have every chance of PASSING YOUR DRIVING TEST.

Reversing into a side road on your left

Drive forwards past the entrance to the side road, remaining in first gear, for a distance of approximately 2-3 car lengths.

Assess the corner as you drive past.

Check mirrors, signal if necessary and bring the car to a stop parallel to, and slightly further away from the kerb than you would for a normal stop – Fig. 1.

Apply the handbrake and select neutral.

If necessary, adjust your seating position (you can remove your seat belt).

Prepare your car for reverse, take all round observations. Wait, if necessary, until it is safe to proceed.

Fig. 1

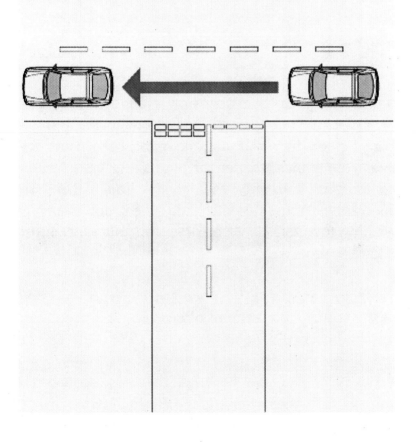

Maintain clutch control to keep car slow, (if reversing down hill use brake to regulate speed of car) whilst looking over left shoulder out of the rear window.

Just before your car reaches the point of turn (where the front of your car will swing out to the right) – Fig. 2, look forwards for oncoming road users and over your right shoulder for overtaking vehicles and pedestrians crossing the road. Look then for pedestrians crossing the side road and vehicles wishing to enter. (If necessary, stop and wait until it is safe to proceed).

Steer towards the left, in accordance with the curve of the corner, (the amount of steering will depend on the sharpness of the corner).

Try and follow the kerb all the way around the corner, by either keeping the kerb in view in the corner of the rear window or within the rear nearside window.

Fig. 2

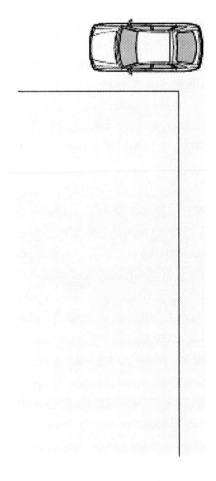

Take all round observation as the car reaches the apex of the corner, being prepared to stop for other road users, if required – Fig. 3.

Also stop and immediately pull forward to the beginning should a vehicle emerge from within the side road.

Maintain a slow speed using clutch control all the way round the corner until the car gets into a position just short of becoming parallel to the left hand kerb – Fig. 4.

Steer back to the right sufficient to straighten up the front wheels, at exactly the same speed and amount as that required to enter the side road.

Continue looking out of the rear window over your left shoulder at the kerb.

Fig. 3

Fig. 4

Check the position of the car to see how far away it is from the kerb and if travelling back parallel with the edge of the kerb.

If necessary, adjust position of car by turning the steering wheel enough to the left or right to line up the car parallel to and within 2 feet (or 60cm.) to the left hand kerb.

Reverse back for 3-4 car lengths from the corner, then bring the car to a stop – Fig. 5.

(Whilst reversing look back to the front for any road user wishing to enter side road, stop if necessary. Vehicles approaching from behind, if they have enough room to pass you and get back to their side of the road before they get to the give-way lines, stop, if not pull back to start).

Fig. 5

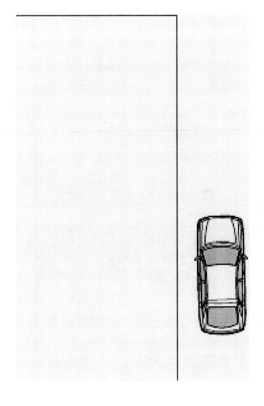

Reversing around a 90 degree corner (left).

To reverse around a 90 degree (right angle) kerb, use the following technique.

Stop in the normal place and prepare your car to move.

Take your observations and move back.

Looking out of side window, wait until the kerb in the side road appears to be 'sitting' on top of the back seat – Fig. 6.

Then take observations before turning the steering wheel *full lock* to the left quickly.

When your car is parallel with the kerb in the side road, straighten the steering wheel (approximately 1.5 turns), and carry on in the usual way.

Fig. 6

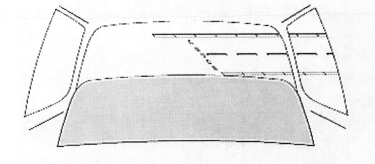

Reversing into a side road on your right.

Continue to drive forwards on the left side of the road until after having passed the side road, remaining in first gear.

Once past the junction, indicate, and move across to the right hand side of the road, stopping approximately 2-3 car lengths past the junction – Fig. 7.

Remember to assess the corner as you drive past the junction.

Check mirrors, signal if necessary, and bring the car to a stop parallel to, and slightly away from the kerb than for a normal stop.

Apply the handbrake and select neutral.

Fig. 7

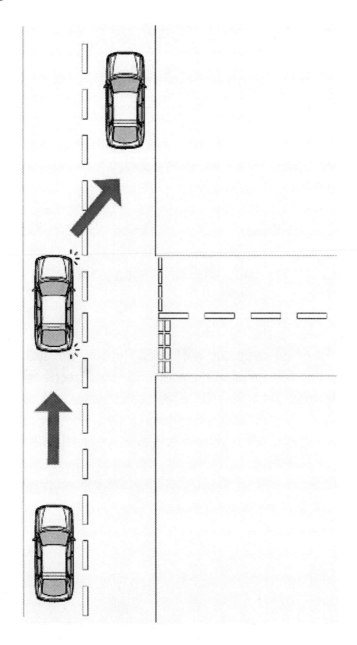

If necessary, remove seatbelt and alter seating position.

Prepare your car for reverse, take all round observations, waiting if necessary until it is safe to proceed.

Maintain clutch control to keep the car slow, (if reversing down hill, use the footbrake to regulate the speed of the car), whilst looking over left shoulder out of rear window.

Just before the car reaches the point of turn (where the front of your car will swing out to the left – Fig. 8), look forwards for oncoming road users and over your left shoulder for passing vehicles. (They may wish to enter the side road), and for pedestrians crossing the road. Also look over your right shoulder for pedestrians wishing to cross the side road and vehicles wishing to exit. (If necessary, stop and wait until it is safe to proceed).

Fig. 8

Now look over right shoulder, and steer towards the right, in accordance with the curve of the corner, (the amount of steering will depend on the sharpness of the corner).

Try and follow the kerb all the way round the corner by keeping the edge in view in the corner of the rear side window.

Take all round observations as the car reaches the apex of the corner, being prepared to stop for other road users if necessary – Fig. 9A.

Maintain a slow speed by using the clutch control all the way round the corner until the car gets into a position just short of becoming parallel to the right hand kerb – Fig. 9B

Steer back to the left sufficient to straighten up the front wheels, at exactly the same speed and amount as that required to enter the side road.

Fig. 9

9A   9B

Now look back over left shoulder out of the rear window.

Check the position of the car to see how far away it is from the kerb and if travelling back parallel to the kerb.

If necessary, adjust the position of the car by turning the steering wheel enough to the left or right to line up the vehicle parallel to and within 2 feet (60 cm.) from the kerb.

Reverse back for 7-8 car lengths from corner, so that you have enough room to drive over to the correct side of the road – Fig. 10, before emerging then bring the car to a stop.

Whilst reversing back in side road, look to the front for any road user wishing to enter, if necessary stop.

Fig. 10

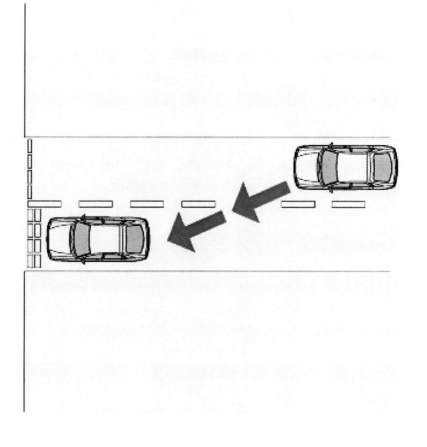

Co-ordination of Controls:

Maintain a slow speed by using clutch control.

The footbrake should be used to regulate the speed of the car when reversing downhill.

The accelerator may require extra pressure when reversing uphill.

Steering wheel, the amount and speed will be dependent on the sharpness of the corner.

Accuracy:

Try and keep reasonably close to the kerb all the way round the corner without touching the kerb or straying over the centre lines of the side road.

Finish parallel to and no more than 2 feet (60 cm.) away from the kerb.

Observations:

All round observations to be taken before commencing and with frequent checks to the front and over the right shoulder, making sure that there are no pedestrians, especially children in the road into which you are reversing.

Stop, if necessary, to allow any following or oncoming vehicles to pass and any pedestrians to cross over behind the car or to cross over the entrance of the side road.

A minimum of 75% of observations should be taken looking out of the rear window with frequent checks to the front and over the right shoulder. The occasional glance in the nearside door mirror is allowed to check distance from the kerb and to see if the car is parallel.

Drivers must be fully aware of any road user throughout this manoeuvre and be prepared to stop, if necessary, to allow them to proceed without hindrance.

Turn in the road

After having carried out a normal stop, prepare car to move.

Take all round observations, if necessary, wait until it is safe to proceed.

Release handbrake and allow the car to crawl using clutch control.

Steer as fast as possible to the right.

As you car approaches the centre of the road check for road users, don't stop for vehicles until you reach the kerb.

Wait until the front of the car almost reaches right angles to the kerb, then steer as much as you can to the left before stopping, making sure you don't overhang kerb – Fig. 11. (If the road slopes towards the kerb push the clutch down and use the brake to regulate the speed of the car).

Fig. 11

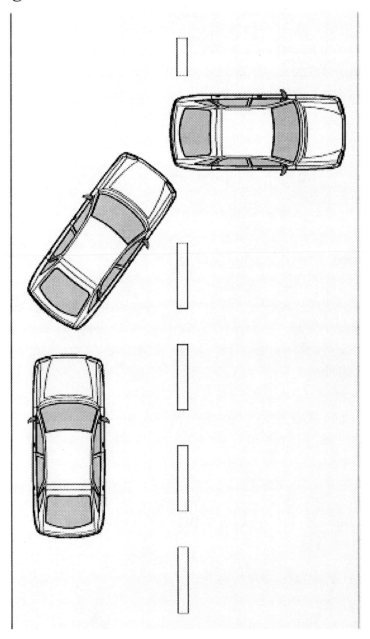

Apply handbrake and immediately select reverse and prepare car to move back.

Take all round observations, allow vehicles to drive past the rear if they wish and pedestrians to walk past your vehicle both front and rear before releasing handbrake.

Make sure approaching drivers have come to a complete stop before moving.

Allow the car to crawl back towards the rear kerb using clutch control. Continue to steer to the left while looking out the rear window over your left shoulder.

As you approach the centre of the road, look over your right shoulder towards the kerb and steer to the right.

Bring the car to a stop before it overhangs the kerb, regulating the speed using the brake if there is a slope – Fig. 12.

Fig. 12

Apply handbrake, immediately select first gear and prepare car to move forward.

Take observations, allow drivers to proceed if they wish, also let pedestrians walk past your car both front and rear before releasing handbrake.

If necessary, steer further to right allowing the car to reach it's driving position before steering left to straighten the front wheels, still using clutch control.

Check all 3 mirrors to make sure it's safe to proceed.

Release the clutch fully and accelerate gently away.

Fig. 13

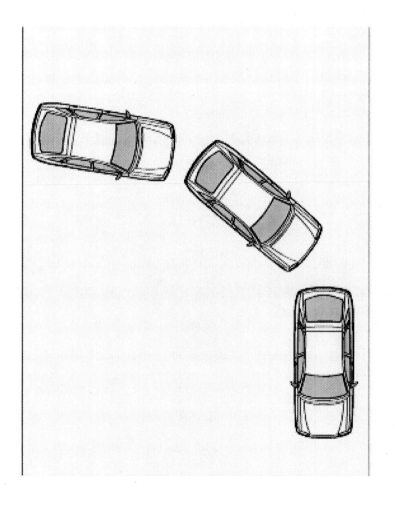

Parallel (reverse) park

Drive forward and stop parallel to, or slightly in front of, parked vehicle, approximately 3 feet (1 metre) from vehicle.

When pulling forward look ahead and check mirror, signal if necessary, and come to a stop alongside – Fig. 14A.

Apply the handbrake and return the gear lever to neutral.

If necessary adjust seating position to get a better view to the rear.

Select reverse and prepare vehicle, take all round observation, waiting if necessary until it is safe to proceed.

Fig. 14A

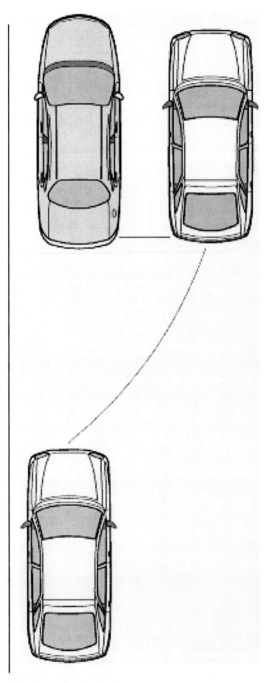

Release handbrake and start to move back slowly using clutch control, while looking through the rear window over your left shoulder, until your vehicle is level with the parked vehicle – Fig, 14A

Fig. 14B

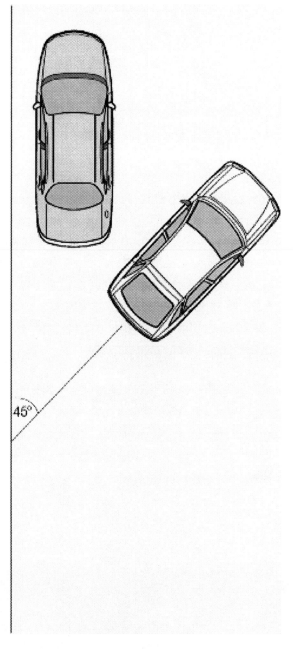

45°

Check all round to make sure it is safe to swing the front of your vehicle out to the right.

While looking out of the rear window turn the steering wheel one full turn (360 degrees) to the left, until you have achieved an angle of approximately 45 degrees towards the kerb at the rear – Fig. 14B.

While waiting for your angle, check that the nearside of your vehicle is not too close to the parked vehicle and take a further look to the front and over your right shoulder for other road users.

Once angle is achieved take that one full turn back off to straighten up the front wheels, allowing the vehicle to roll back to the kerb. If the road slopes towards the kerb use the footbrake to regulate the speed of the vehicle – Fig. 15.

Fig. 15

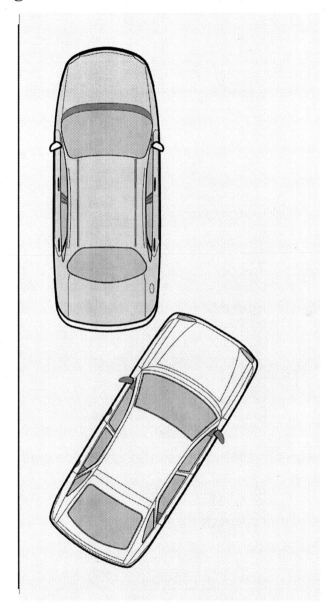

Looking out the rear window at the kerb, it will look like the kerb is moving across the back window – Fig. 16.

Once the kerb is behind driver, turn the steering wheel further to the right onto full lock, if necessary, to swing the front of the vehicle in towards the kerb – Fig. 17. Stop when the vehicle is parallel.

Remember to apply the handbrake between gear changes. If not quite parallel or too far away from the kerb you are allowed one pull forward and one reverse.

Alternatively:

Carry on as above until you have straightened the wheels – Fig. 15. You can wait until the front nearside corner of your vehicle has safely cleared the extremity of the parked vehicle, before steering to the right on to full lock, if necessary, to swing the front of the vehicle in towards the kerb.

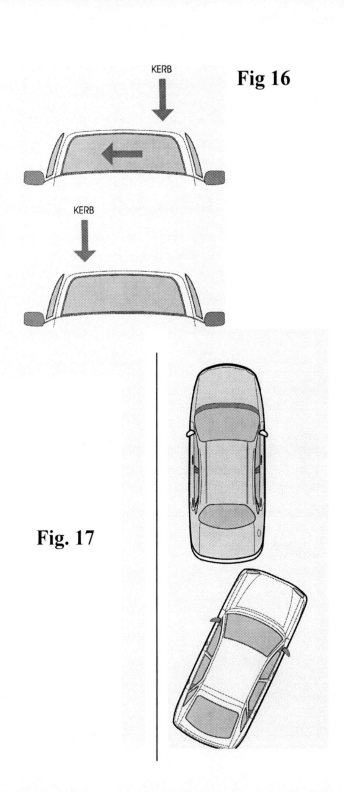

KERB

Fig 16

KERB

Fig. 17

Another option:

Carry on as above until you have taken the full turn back off to straighten the front wheels – Fig. 14B.

Wait until the rear of your vehicle gets in line with the nearside lights of the parked vehicle – Fig. 19, then swing vehicle in towards the kerb. Stop when parallel.

Another option:

Carry on as above until you have completed the one full turn to the left – Fig. 14A.

Wait until the passenger door mirror gets in line with the rear of the parked vehicle – Fig. 18.

Turn the steering wheel enough to the right to swing the front of your vehicle in towards the kerb. Stop when parallel.

Fig. 18

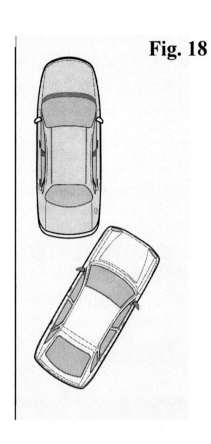

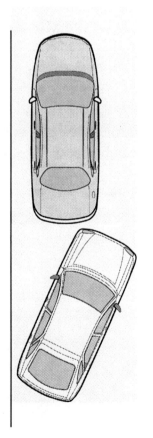

Fig. 19

Accuracy:

Before commencing, it should be noted that our finishing position should be no more than 2 car lengths from the object vehicle and no more than 1 foot (20 cm) from the kerb. We should also make sure that the car is parallel to the kerb.

Co-ordination of Controls:

Maintain a slow speed by using clutch control.

Footbrake should be used to regulate the speed on the camber should one exist, or if the car picks up too much speed.

Steering wheel will only require minimum amounts of turn to the right or left at the appropriate stages of the manoeuvre.

Observations:

All round observations should be taken before commencing and at appropriate stages of this manoeuvre.

Stop, if necessary, to allow pedestrians to pass by on the pavement, and for any vehicles to drive past from the front or rear.

A minimum of 75% of observations should be taken looking out of the rear window over the left shoulder, with frequent checks to the front and over the right shoulder.

Use of the nearside door mirror should be restricted to the occasional glance to check position and determine whether car is parallel to kerb.

Mirrors

Rear View - Used not only to see what is behind you but how close, before braking.

Never let the following traffic get too close to you. If they do, ease off your gas pedal very slowly so that the following vehicles will drop back.

Left Door - To make sure that there are no cyclists or people too close to the side of your car before signalling to the left.

Right Door - To make sure there are no vehicles overtaking you before signalling to the right.

Blind Spots - Remember these have to be checked. These are areas not covered by mirrors.

Signals - To be given when it is both safe and clear. Also to inform other road users what you are about to do.

Don't give misleading signals.

Weather

Sunshine - Can dazzle you. If this happens, divert your eyes to the side of the road so you can still follow the road without swerving.

You can also slow down or even come to a stop at a safe place.

Roads become very slippery if it rains after a long, dry spell.

Rain - Can reduce visibility and the grip your tyres have on the road surface.

It will take you, and everyone else, longer to come to a stop.

It will also increase the chance of skidding.

Slow down, or even stop, until visibility improves.

Mud - Reduces tyre grip on the road.

Wind -	Will cause cyclists, motorcyclists and high-sided vehicles to swerve, maybe in front of you.
	Look out for people standing near the kerb, they may be blown onto the road.
Snow/Ice -	Tyres lose grip.
	It takes much longer to stop. You should allow at least 10 times the normal stopping distance.
	If your journey is necessary, take care and reduce speed.
Fog -	If your trip is essential, reduce speed and the distance from the vehicle in front.
	Never drive too close following their brake lights.

Roundabouts

What you have to remember is a roundabout is just another junction which keeps the traffic moving.

The following guides you to take roundabouts with relative ease, including the mini-roundabout, or those represented by a painted disc on the road.

At double roundabouts, treat the two separately, not as one.

The mirror-signal-manoeuvre-position-speed-look routine should still be applied here as at any other junction. Similarly, signals for left and right turns should be given in plenty of time so that other drivers know your intentions early.

The general rule when approaching roundabouts is that you give way to traffic approaching from your right so as not to make them slow down or swerve, but if clear keep moving.

Long vehicles and buses may require more room dependant on the shape and size of the roundabout. Their position may appear wrong to you.

Be careful if you approach behind cyclists or horse and riders as they may go round the outside, even if going completely round.

Treat the roundabout as if it were a 'clock face', where you approach from the 6 o'clock position with the 12 o'clock being the road opposite. To take any road that leaves the roundabout from the 6 o'clock *up* to the 12 o'clock position (inclusive) approach it in the left hand lane. Therefore, when taking any road from the 12 o'clock position, *down* to the 6 o'clock position, the approach to the roundabout should be the right hand lane – Fig. 20.

Fig. 20

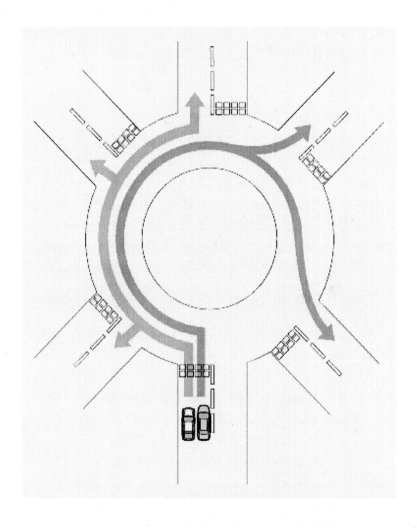

Where there are two or more lanes at the entrance there may be road markings – Fig. 22, or signs indicating which lane to select. Where there is only one lane at the entrance take the most convenient lane suitable for the exit you wish to take.

If leaving by the first exit, signal left on approach and keep to that lane. Take observations on approach and decide if you can carry on or if you have to stop – Fig. 21.

If leaving by the second exit or following the road ahead, no signal is required, but you still keep to the left hand lane on approach and throughout, signalling to leave once level with the exit before the one to be taken – Fig. 21.

Make sure that you do not cut into the path of traffic on your right hand lane.

If leaving by an exit on your right, approach in the right hand lane giving right turn indicator. Keep to this lane throughout, still signalling right – Fig. 20, until you are level with the exit before the one to be taken. Then change the signal to the left and leave on the left hand side of the exit road unless road markings indicate otherwise.

Fig. 21

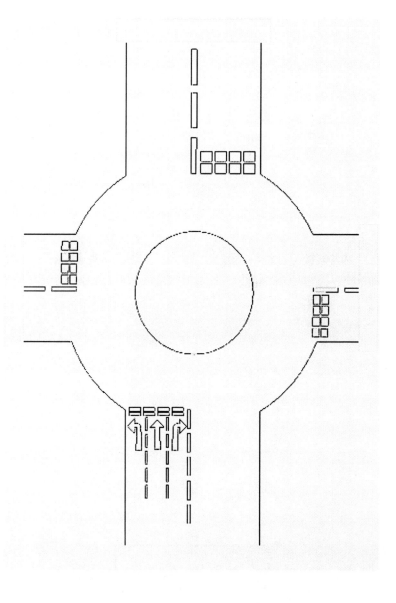

Where there are only 3 roads at a roundabout – Fig. 22, with two lanes on approach, the left lane is best for the first exit and the right lane for the second exit.

Fig. 22

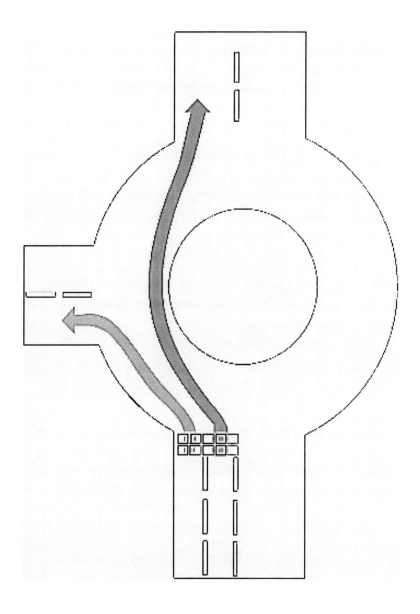

Pedestrian Crossings

The first thing to do is identify the crossing.

Flashing Belisha beacons on top of back and white striped poles signify a zebra crossing.

For all other crossings there will be a yellow box attached to the poles to enable pedestrians to press the button and activate the system.

Use the MSM (mirror-signal-manoeuvre) routine on the approach to see if you can continue, or if you have to come to a stop.

All have zigzag lines on approach within which you should *never* park or overtake the vehicle in front.

Always keep crossings clear.

Never, 'invite' pedestrians to cross – Fig. 23, rev. your engine, sound your horn, or edge forwards.

Fig. 23

Fig. 24

Look out for pedestrians already crossing, or those wishing to cross.

Approach at a speed that will enable you to stop, if necessary, to give way to pedestrians.

You must stop whenever pedestrians have stepped onto the crossing.

Stop the car behind the give-way lines, or any other vehicle already stopped.

If the crossing has a central traffic island in the middle of the road, it can be treated as two separate crossings – Fig. 25.

Once pedestrians have passed in front of your car, watch out for pedestrians who may rush across before traffic starts to move.

Drive on when safe.

Fig 24

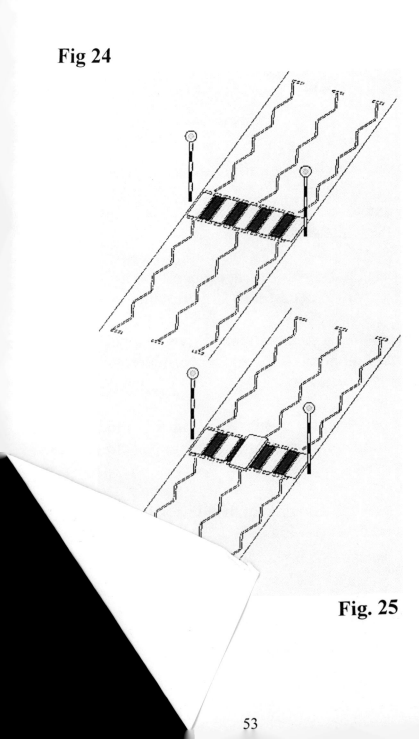

Fig. 25

Pelican Crossings

Fig. 26

These are controlled by traffic lights.

When amber or red lights appear you must stop behind the white stop line.

When the 'flashing amber' appears on the lights, you must give way to pedestrians still crossing.

If the crossing is clear you may drive on, checking to make sure nobody is going to rush across before traffic starts to move.

If there is a central traffic island in the middle and the crossing is in a straight line, then this is treated as one crossing – Fig. 27

If the crossing is staggered, then this is treated as two separate crossings – Fig. 28.

Fig. 26

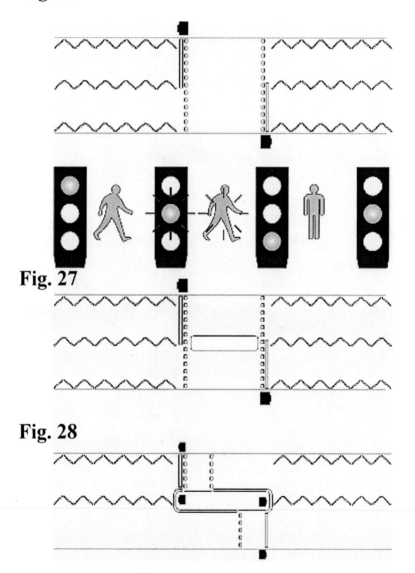

Fig. 27

Fig. 28

Puffin Crossings

These are controlled by traffic lights.

This type of crossing has an 'infrared detector' which senses that pedestrians wish to use, or are still using, the crossing which keeps a red light showing towards motorists.

There is no 'flashing amber' and the lights immediately change to green.

Check to ensure nobody is going to rush across before the traffic starts to move, Fig. 30.

Fig. 29

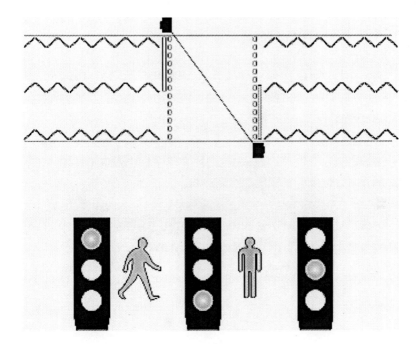

Fig. 30

Toucan Crossings

These are controlled by traffic lights.

They differ in that both pedestrians and cyclists can cross at the same time, without cyclists having to dismount.

Similar to Puffin Crossings, red changes directly to green with no 'flashing amber'.

Check both sides of the crossing for anyone rushing to cross before traffic starts to move.

Fig. 31

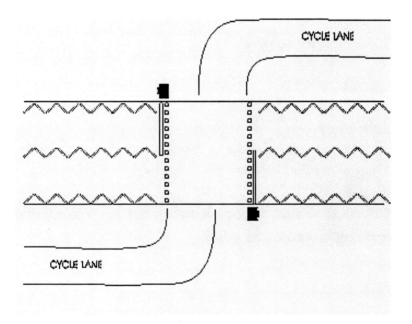

School Crossings

Fig. 32

You must obey all signals given by the 'Lollipop Person' and must wait until the patrol has lowered the sign and walked off the road before proceeding.

Take extra care before moving off for youngsters rushing to cross the road.

Fig. 32

Meet Approaching Traffic

Use MSM (mirror-signal-manoeuvre) and assess the oncoming traffic.

Decide which vehicle has priority and try to judge what action the oncoming driver intends to take.

Give way when the left side of the road is obstructed, or when oncoming vehicles are already committed to driving past obstructions on their side of the road.

Look for a safe place to stop and let oncoming vehicles proceed.

Meeting Traffic at Night

The lights of oncoming vehicles tells you their direction of travel, but very little of speed.

Ask yourself:-

How far away is he and how fast is he approaching?

Is this the sort of road where I should slow down or stop while we pass each other?

Remember pedestrians and cyclists are also hard to see.

Anticipation of Drivers

Look ahead on both sides of the road for any signs of other drivers giving any sign that they are going to change direction or speed.

Watch out for BRAKELIGHTS – INDICATORS – HAZARDS - REVERSING LIGHTS.

Use the MSM (mirror-signal-manoeuvre) routine.

Decide and act on this information by adjusting the SPEED and/or POSITION of your vehicle, return to normal position as soon as possible.

In anticipation lies the answer to most of the questions a driver must always be asking themself, such as:

WHAT AM I LIKELY TO FIND?

WHAT IS HE GOING TO DO?

SHOULD I SLOW DOWN, OR SPEED UP?

SHOULD I STOP? WHERE EXACTLY? etc.

Anticipation of Pedestrians

When pedestrians are observed on the road ahead, use the MSM (mirror-signal-manoeuvre) routine before adjusting road position or speed.

Approach at a speed that you can stop if necessary.

Give sufficient room to the pedestrians before proceeding.

Anticipation of Cyclists

When cyclists are viewed on the road ahead, use the MSM (mirror-signal-manoeuvre) routine before attempting to pass.

Give at least 6 feet (4-5 metres) clearance while driving past.

Wait until you can see the cyclist in your rear view mirror before moving back in.

Overtaking

When overtaking other vehicles you must make sure it is going to be safe.

Decide if it is necessary.

Decide if it is a suitable place and time.

Decide if you have enough room to get back to your own side of the road, after overtaking, without making any other vehicle swerve or slow down.

GET THESE WRONG AND YOU ARE IN SERIOUS DANGER OF BEING INVOLVED IN AN ACCIDENT, WHICH CAN CAUSE SERIOUS INJURY OR EVEN DEATH.

Before we discuss the routine for overtaking, one little warning, BE CAREFUL. Some drivers seem to think because the vehicle in front of them has overtaken, it is safe for them to follow. The vehicle in front will not protect you. The driver has plenty of time to get back to his side of the road leaving you in 'danger'.

Mirror -   To check if safe and clear.

Position - Close enough so you get a good view of the road ahead and you can   overtake smoothly.

Speed -   Enough to pass quickly and get back to your side of the road. You may have to change down to a lower gear for extra speed.

Look -   Assess any type of hazard. The speed of the vehicle you are overtaking.

Mirrors -   To make sure the road is still safe and clear in front, behind and at the sides of your vehicle.

Signal -   If necessary, to inform other road users what you are about to do.

Manoeuvre -Pull out and pass as safely and quickly as possible. Wait until you can see the vehicle which you have overtaken in your rear view mirror before returning to your side of the road, to avoid 'cutting him up'.

Remember, if in doubt – **DON'T**.

Motorways

Motorways are by far the safest roads to use because there are less hazards.

Plan your journey so you know where to join and leave the motorway, allowing plenty of time for any delays and rests in motorway service stations.

TIREDNESS KILLS.

When joining motorways you need to firstly build up your speed on the slip road to match that of the vehicles on the motorway.

Don't assume the other vehicles will 'give way' to you to let you join the traffic by slowing down or moving across to the next lane, they don't have to.

If you cannot join, then you must be prepared to slow down or even stop.

Once on the motorway you must be able to keep up with the flow of traffic so as not to hold them up.

When passing other slip roads and seeing there are vehicles wishing to join the traffic flow, see if it is safe for you to change lanes to let them out, or maybe slow down. Remember they might not slow down once they have reached the end of the slip road, then what would you do?

Overtaking on Motorways

Because of the higher speed limit, you need to make sure you have enough space and time to overtake and get back into the left without 'cutting in'.

Because of the higher speed limit, accidents tend to be more serious when they occur. You must be able to 'read the road' well ahead of you so you can see what is happening. You should also drive at a speed that will enable you to stop well within the distance you can see to be clear, (i.e. between you and the car in front).

Drive also at a speed suitable for the road conditions (e.g. fog, heavy rain, etc.).

Slow down, you will still reach your destination..... safely.

When leaving the motorway, check your speed as you may be travelling faster than you think.

The Driving Test

Before applying for the driving test, you must sit and pass the 'Theory Test' first.

The vehicle you are sitting your test in must:-

- Be in a roadworthy condition, also taxed and insured with a current M.O.T. certificate, the speedometer must be in MPH and not kilometres.

- Be fitted with "L" plates ('D' plates in Wales), visible from the front and rear of the vehicle.

- Be fitted with a seatbelt, headrest and a small interior mirror for use by the examiner.

If these conditions are not complied with, the test may be cancelled and the fee lost.

There is no Pass/Fail quota. If you show the examiner you have good control of the vehicle and do not make any serious or dangerous mistakes, you should pass your driving test.

The reason most people fail is because they are simply not ready or prepared enough. Nerves do play a part, but if you listen to the advice given by your instructor, or given in this book, you will have every chance of passing.

On the day of your test make sure you arrive at the test centre in plenty of time, most centres will allow a little time for being late (check with centre), whatever the cause. Failure to do so may mean the test is cancelled and the fee lost.

The test lasts for approximately 40 minutes.

When it is time the examiner will enter the waiting room and call your name. He will ask you to read and sign a declaration saying the vehicle is insured.

He will then ask you to lead the way to your vehicle. On the way he will get you to read, with glasses if worn, a vehicle's number plate approximately 25 yards (20.5 metres) away. New style number plates will be read at a shorter distance.

You will also be asked two questions, one SHOW ME, and one TELL ME, relating to the safety of your vehicle (A list can be found at the end of this chapter)

Ignore what the examiner is doing, or marking, as this is quite normal and may not affect the outcome.

Remember the examiner will not ask you to do anything that you should not have learnt.

If you have made a mistake during the test, rectify it if possible and carry on as normal.

Don't try to impress the examiner, just concentrate on driving at an appropriate speed for the road and weather conditions, attend to smooth use of controls.

Take proper action when meeting other road users, pedestrians, cyclists, horses and riders.

In each of the following the examiner will ask you to pull in and park at a safe place, then explain what to do.

- The Emergency Stop:-
  Not everyone will be given this, only 1 in 3 vehicles. Try not to skid, if you do rectify it. Try not to stall the vehicle.

You will also be asked to do 2 manoeuvres out of the following:-

- Reverse:-
  Normally into a side road on your left, (unless you are driving a van or vehicle with limited visibility, in which case you will be given a side road on your right), you must be able to do both.

- Turn in the Road:-
  By making the vehicle face the opposite direction using forward and reverse gears. Try not to overhang the kerb or touch the kerb with your tyres.

- Reverse park (Parallel Park):-
  By pulling alongside a parked vehicle and reversing back in, if the situation arises you may be asked to park in between 2 parked cars. You may even be asked to reverse into a parking bay at the test centre if there is one there.

After the test the examiner will tell you if you have passed, or if you failed they will tell you where you went wrong.

Once you have passed your driving test you will be put on 'probation' for 2 years. This means if you get 6 penalty points within this time you will be put back to a leaner and have to sit both tests all over again.

You may wish to further your driving career by taking 'Pass Plus' (visit www.passplus.org.uk), which is a course designed to accelerate the learning process. (It can also lead to a discount on your car insurance), or you can take a course in advanced driving.

Safety Check Questions for Cars

Q. Open the bonnet, identify where you would check the engine oil level and TELL ME how you would check the engine has enough oil.

A. Identify dipstick / oil level indicator, describe check of oil level against minimum / maximum markers, describe how to top up.

Q. SHOW ME how you would check that the power assisted steering is working.

A. Gentle pressure on the steering wheel while the engine is started should result in a slight but noticeable movement as the system begins to operate. If the steering becomes heavy the system may not be working.

Q. Open the bonnet, identify where you would check the engine coolant level and TELL ME how you would check the engine has the correct amount.

A. Identify high / low level markings on header tank or radiator filler cap and describe how to top up level.

Q. SHOW ME how you would check the hand-break for excessive wear.

A. Demonstrate by applying. When applied it secures itself and does not come up too high.

Q. Identify where the windscreen washer reservoir is and TELL ME how you would check the level.

A. Identify reservoir and explain how to check level.

Q. SHOW ME how you would check the horn is working.

A. Identify / press horn (turn on ignition if necessary).

Q. Open the bonnet, identify where the brake fluid reservoir is and TELL ME how you would check the level

A. Identify reservoir and check against high / low markings.

Q. SHOW ME how you would check the brake lights are working.

A. Press pedal, ask someone to check or use reflections on windows etc..

Q. SHOW ME how you would check the indicators are working.

A. Apply indicators / hazards and walk round the vehicle

Q. TELL ME how you would check the brakes are working.

A Brakes should not feel spongy or slack or pull to one side.

Q. SHOW ME how you would check that the headlights / tail lights are working.

A. Operate switch (turn on ignition if necessary), walk round vehicle.

Q. TELL ME how you would check the tyres to ensure they have enough tread depth and their condition is roadworthy.

A. Must have minimum 1.6 mm of tread depth across the central ¾ of the breath of the tyre and around the entire circumference. Free from cuts and bulges.

Q. TELL ME where you would find the information for the recommended tyre pressures for the car and check them

A. Car hand-book. Use a reliable pressure gauge, check when cold. Don't forget the spare tyre. Remember to refit valve caps.

TIPS

- There is no such thing as a 'dangerous road'.....it is the driver who is to blame, by lack of 'forward planning' (not looking far enough ahead to see what you are approaching).

- Having had an argument with someone, not feeling well, taking certain medication will all affect your concentration and your reaction time which may cause you to have an accident. Avoid driving in these circumstances.

- Expect the unexpected – don't think others will do the correct thing – they probably won't.

- The secret of being a good driver is to know what is around you at any time.

- Finding emergency stop distances (in feet) will be easy if you use the following technique. As you know they are broken down into 3 categories:- Thinking Distance, Breaking Distance and Overall Stopping Distance. Your thinking distance is always your speed you are travelling at. To find your approximate breaking distance:

start at 20 mph and multiply by 1.
at 30 mph multiply by 1½
at 40 mph multiply by 2
Keep adding ½ for every 10 mph increase.
Then to find your Overall Stopping Distance add together the Thinking Distance and your approximate Breaking Distance (see Table).

Speed	Thinking Distance	Multiply by	Breaking Distance	Stopping Distance (TD + BD)
20	20	1	20	40
30	30	1.5	45	75
40	40	2	80	120
50	50	2.5	125	175
60	60	3	180	240
70	70	3.5	245	315

- Only use 'fog lights' when your visibility is seriously reduced, 109 yards/100 metres or less.

  Remember to switch them off when visibility improves.

- When approaching traffic lights or pedestrian crossings, remember to approach at a speed at which you can stop safely.

- Drive at a speed that you can stop safely within the distance you can see to be clear (The 2 second Rule). Remember on wet or icy roads it will take you longer to come to a stop, increase your distance accordingly.

- Any time you stop behind another vehicle, be sure you can see the bottom of his rear wheels and some of the road. That way, should the vehicle in front break down, you will still have enough room to move around him.

Fig. 33

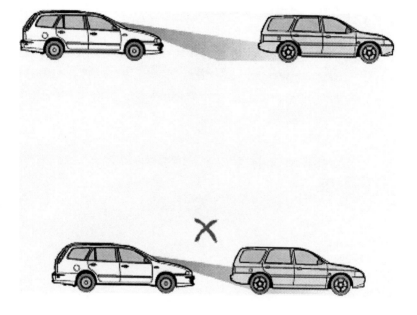

- Under inflated and over inflated tyres can overheat and may cause a 'blow out' (explode). They will also affect the car's handling and increase wear on the suspension. The tyres will wear out more quickly and you will use more fuel. If you do get a 'blow out', keep feet clear of pedals, hold the steering wheel firmly and let the car roll to a stop.

- Tyres must have a tread depth of 1.6mm over three quarters of the tyre and it's entire circumference. It must also be free from cuts and defects.

Do not mix cross ply and radials on same axle.

Safe Parking

Figs. 34, 35, 36 & 37

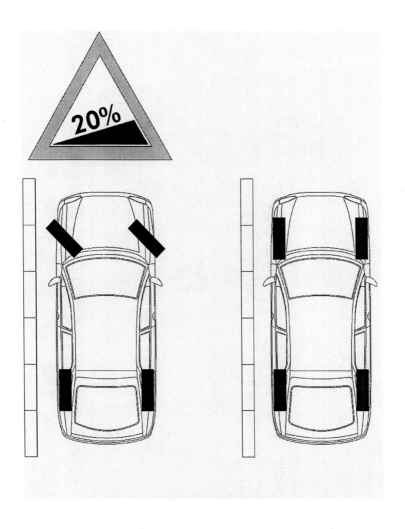

Figs: 36 & 37

if facing uphill select first gear and if facing downhill select reverse gear.

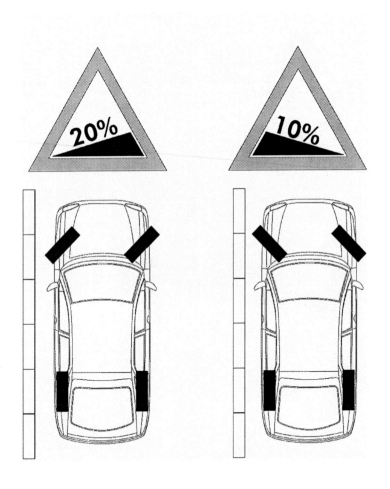

Accident Report Form

Date: Time: Weather:

Location: Road Width:

Other vehicle: Make:
    Model:
                         Colour:
    Registration No.:

Apparent damage:

Driver's name:

Driver's address:

Number of passengers:

Any apparent injuries:

Other property damage:

Police in attendance: PC Number:

Witnesses:

(Also a sketch is required with a photograph(s) on back).

PLANNED PROGRAMME OF TUITION

	NAME	INSTRUCTED	TRY AGAIN	GOOD	MOCK TEST
	Licence				
	Eyesight				
01	**COCKPIT DRILL – D.S.S.M.S.**				
02	**CONTROLS**				
03	**PRECAUTIONS** before starting engine				
04	**MOVING OFF SAFELY**				
	Prep – Observation - Manoeuvre				
	Level				
	Uphill				
	Downhill				
	Enough Gas				
	Smooth Clutch				
05	**STOPPING SAFELY**				
	Mirrors – Signal – Manoeuvre				
	Progressive Braking				
	Close to Kerb				
	Safe and Convenient				
06	**CHANGING GEARS UP**				
	In Time				
	Smooth Clutch				
07	**CHANGING GEARS DOWN**				
	In Time				

	Smooth Clutch				
	Not Coasting				
	2 to 1 Uphill				
08	**STEERING**				
	Technique				
	Positioning				
09	**CLUTCH CONTROL**				
	Level				
	Uphill				
10	**MOVING OFF AT AN ANGLE**				
	Level				
	Uphill				
	Downhill				
11	**EMERGENCY STOP**				
	Under Control				
	Moving Off Safely				
12	**TURNING LEFT - MAJOR TO MINOR**				
	Mirrors				
	Signal				
	Position				
	Speed				
	Gear				
	Clutch				
	Observation				
	Turning				
13	**TURNING LEFT – MINOR TO MAJOR**				
	Mirrors				
	Signal				
	Position				
	Speed				
	Gear				
	When to Stop/Proceed				
	Handbrake if Necessary				
	Observation				

	Turning				
14	**TURNING RIGHT – MAJOR TO MINOR**				
	Mirrors				
	Signal				
	Position				
	Speed				
	Gear				
	Clutch				
	Observation				
	Turning				
15	**TURNING RIGHT - MINOR TO MAJOR**				
	Mirrors				
	Signal				
	Position				
	Speed				
	Gear				
	When to Stop/Proceed				
	Handbrake if Necessary				
	Observation				
	Turning				
16	**UNMARKED CROSSROADS**				
17	**ZONES OF VISION**				
	Restricted – Slow/Stop/Creep				
	Early View - Progress				
18	**REVERSE LEFT/RIGHT**				
	Observations				
	Control				
	Turning Points				
	Straightening				
	Accuracy				
19	**REVERSE LEFT/RIGHT**				
	Observations				
	Control				
	Turning Points				

	Straightening					
	Accuracy					
20	**TURN IN THE ROAD**					
	Observations					
	Control					
	Energetic Steering					
	Steering Back					
	Accuracy					
	x 3 x 5					
21	**REVERSE PARKING**					
	Observations					
	Control					
	Turning Points					
	Straightening					
	Accuracy					
	Two Cars					
22	MIRRORS WELL BEFORE					
	Moving Off					
	Signalling					
	Overtaking					
	Changing Lanes					
	Slowing Down					
	Stopping					
	Opening Door					
23	**GIVE SIGNALS**					
	Where Necessary					
	In Good Time					
24	**CARE IN THE USE OF SPEED**					
	Observe Limits					
	Road and Traffic Conditions					
25	**MAKE PROGRESS**					
	Without Hesitation					
	Soon Up Through Gears					
	Road and Traffic Conditions					
26	**ROAD POSITIONING**					
	Keep Left					

	Lane Discipline				
	Adequate Clearance				
27	**ROUNDABOUTS**				
	Mirrors				
	Signals				
	Position				
	Observation				
	Speed				
	Gears				
28	**TRAFFIC LIGHTS**				
	Approaching on Red				
	Approaching on Green				
	Stopping – 1st. Gear				
	Handbrake – Ready				
	Check Before Moving Off				
	Turning Left/Filter				
	Turning Right				
29	**PEDESTRIAN CROSSINGS**				
	Approaching				
	Stopping – 1st. Gear				
	Handbrake – Ready				
	Moving Off Safely				
30	**APPROACHING HAZARDS**				
	Mirrors – Signal – Manoeuvre				
	Stay Low/Change Down				
31	**MEET OTHER VEHICLES**				
	Mirrors – Signal – Manoeuvre				
	Slow/Stop				
	Position				
	Adequate Clearance				
32	**CROSS THE PATH OF OTHER VEHICLES**				
	Mirrors – Signal – Manoeuvre				
	Position				
	Matching Speed				
	Adequate Clearance				

	Check New Road Clear				
33	**OVERTAKE**				
	Mirrors – Signal – Manoeuvre				
	Check Clear Ahead				
	Use of Gears/Gas				
	Observe Speed Limits				
	Adequate Clearance				
34	**NIGHT DRIVING**				
35	**ALL WEATHER DRIVING**				
36	**SIGNS AND ROAD MARKINGS**				
	Notice Every Sign/Marking				
	Drive by Direction Signs Only				
37	**AWARENESS AND ANTICIPATION**				
	Vehicles (Signals)				
	Motor/Cyclists (Signals)				
	Pedestrians				
38	**READING THE ROAD**				
	Look Well Ahead				
	Give Commentary				
39	**DUAL CARRIAGEWAYS**				
	Use of Speed				
	Motorways (Theory)				
40	**MOCK TEST**				
41	**HIGHWAY CODE**				
42	**REMEDIAL**				
43	**PRETEST/TEST**				
44	**MOTORWAY DRIVING**				
	Joining				
	Adequate Space				
	Lane Discipline				
	Use of Speed				
	Overtaking				
	Leaving Motorway				
	VIDEOS LENT				

NOTES;					
APPLICATION DATE					
TEST DATE					

Own Notes

Breinigsville, PA USA
08 January 2010
230452BV00003B/48/A